On the Job

Police Officers
In Our Community

Michelle Ames

PowerKiDS press.

New York

To my dad, a great police officer

Published in 2010 by The Rosen Publishing Group, Inc.
29 East 21st Street, New York, NY 10010

Copyright © 2010 by The Rosen Publishing Group, Inc.

First Edition

Editor: Nicole Pristash
Book Design: Greg Tucker
Photo Research: Jessica Gerweck

Photo Credits: Cover, pp. 9, 11, 13, 15, 17, 19, 24 Shutterstock.com; p. 5 UpperCut Images/Getty Images; p. 7 © www.iStockphoto.com/Daniel Loiselle; p. 21 Getty Images; p. 23 Darrin Klimek/Getty Images.

Library of Congress Cataloging-in-Publication Data

Ames, Michelle.
  Police officers in our community / Michelle Ames. — 1st ed.
      p. cm. — (On the job)
  Includes index.
  ISBN 978-1-4042-8057-1 (library binding) — ISBN 978-1-4358-2453-9 (pbk.) — ISBN 978-1-4358-2464-5 (6-pack)
  1. Police—Juvenile literature. I. Title.
  HV7922.A465 2010
  363.2—dc22
                                        2008048148

Contents

This is a police officer. A police officer's job is to help keep people safe.

While on the job, a police officer drives a police car.

An officer gets calls for help on a police radio.

Police officers help when an **accident** has happened.

When a person has broken the law, a police officer takes him to **jail**.

A police officer stops people from driving too fast.

This officer is riding a police **motorcycle**.

When there is a **crowd** of people, police officers ride horses. The officers can see if there is trouble in the crowd.

Sometimes, a police officer works with a police dog.

A police officer is important because she helps people every day.

Words to Know

accident

crowd

jail

motorcycle

Index

Web Sites

Due to the changing nature of Internet links, PowerKids Press has developed an online list of Web sites related to the subject of this book. This site is updated regularly. Please use this link to access the list:

www.powerkidslinks.com/job/police/

24